MEG and MOG
Four Plays
for Children

Also by David Wood

ROALD DAHL'S THE BFG: PLAYS FOR CHILDREN (adapt)

David Wood

Four Plays
for Children

Based on Meg and Mog books by
Helen Nicoll and Jan Pieńkowski

PUFFIN BOOKS

PUFFIN BOOKS

Published by the Penguin Group
Penguin Books Ltd, 27 Wrights Lane, London w8 5tz, England
Penguin Books USA Inc., 375 Hudson Street, New York, New York 10014, USA
Penguin Books Australia Ltd, Ringwood, Victoria, Australia
Penguin Books Canada Ltd, 10 Alcorn Avenue, Toronto, Ontario, Canada m4v 3b2
Penguin Books (NZ) Ltd, 182–190 Wairau Road, Auckland 10, New Zealand

Penguin Books Ltd, Registered Offices: Harmondsworth, Middlesex, England

First published 1994
9 10 8

Filmset by Datix International Limited, Bungay, Suffolk
Printed in England by Clays Ltd, St Ives plc
Set in 14/15 pt Monophoto Garamond

CONTENTS

For my four special Unicorn Megs – Maureen Lipman, Amanda Barrie, Sarah Greene and Leni Harper, with love and thanks.

D. W.

These plays are adapted from *Meg and Mog Show*, David Wood's full-length stage adaptation of *Meg and Mog* books by Helen Nicoll and Jan Pieńkowski, originally commissioned by Unicorn Theatre and published by Samuel French Limited.

The plays are based on: *Meg and Mog, Meg's Eggs, Meg's Castle, Meg on the Moon* and *Mog at the Zoo*.

INTRODUCTION

Plays for very young children to perform
need to involve a large group or a whole
class, or, indeed, a whole 'year', without
giving any one child too much responsibility.
For children who don't want to act there
needs to be a variety of other jobs – musicians, stage-managers, puppeteers or sound-
effects makers. It should be possible for
children themselves, helped by adults –
parents, teachers or older friends – to make
scenery, props and costumes without need
of too much technical skill or know-how.
A storyteller (most probably an adult) needs
to hold the performance together. There
should be opportunities for the audience to join
in the fun. The plays should not be too long.
There should be no need for stage lighting.
Music should be playable on improvised
instruments.

I hope that the *Meg and Mog Plays* fulfil these criteria and offer fun and enjoyment for participants and audience alike. I have purposely made each play in the sequence a little more demanding than its predecessor. But nothing should tax too much the enthusiasm of a young cast and the patience of a helpful adult director.

David Wood

MEG AND THE STEGOSAURUS

THE PEOPLE IN THE PLAY

STAGE-MANAGERS, who carry on the cutout scenery and hold it during the scenes

MUSICIANS/SOUND-EFFECTS MAKERS, with various percussion instruments, whistles and other 'noises'

STORYTELLER. Probably an adult, or several children dividing the lines between them

MEG, the witch

MOG, Meg's cat

OWL, Meg's owl

CUCKOO CLOCK

STEGOSAURUS, a hungry prehistoric beast

PUPPETEERS to operate shadow puppets of
   1 MEG and MOG
   2 OWL
   3 TESS ⎫
   4 JESS ⎬ witches
   5 BESS ⎪
   6 CRESS ⎭

TESS
JESS   } witches
BESS
CRESS

FROG
BEETLE   } ingredients for a spell
BAT
SPIDER

MOUSE 1
MOUSE 2
MOUSE 3
MOUSE 4

FLOWERS and VEGETABLES. As many children as possible dressed as, or carrying, cutout props of flowers and vegetables

SCENERY AND PROPS

These should, in the main, be simple cutouts painted in bright, primary colours as in the *Meg and Mog* books' illustrations by Jan Pieńkowski.

A stage is not necessary. In a classroom or school hall, for example, two simple screens or curtains can provide masking for STEGOSAURUS, the WITCHES and the MICE when necessary.

ingredients on
props table

screen   screen

cutout
cauldron

ACTING AREA

plus musicians and storyteller

AUDIENCE

The BED is an
upright cutout,
held by two
STAGE-MANAGERS
behind which
MEG, MOG and
OWL can stand.

The CUCKOO-CLOCK
is a cutout, behind
which the CUCKOO
hides his or her head
until the appropriate
moment; then the head
can appear through the
clock face, which
would open outwards.
Alternatively the
head could peep
round the side.

The CAULDRON is a cutout, self-standing, big enough to conceal STEGOSAURUS crouching behind. Its position should overlap slightly the screen behind, allowing the INGREDIENTS to 'climb' in by simply going round the back, ducking down inside and then crawling behind the screen. The STEGOSAURUS can delay his move to behind the cauldron until the last possible moment before he reveals himself.

Three EGGS, FISH, JAM, a bottle of MILK, a loaf of BREAD, a spoonful of COCOA – all cut-outs.

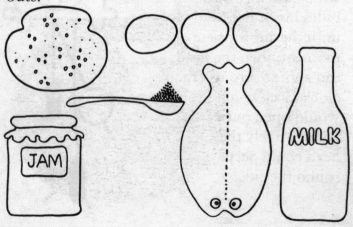

BROOMSTICKS for the witches.

SHADOW PUPPETS of

2 OWL

1 MEG and MOG

(cutouts attached to rods)

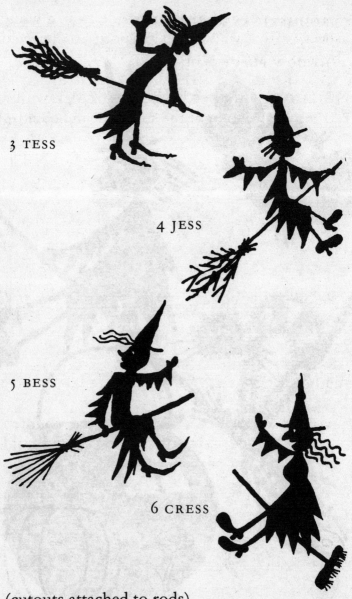

3 TESS

4 JESS

5 BESS

6 CRESS

(cutouts attached to rods)

SHADOW-PUPPET SCREEN, made from a white sheet, with two vertical supports, to be held by two STAGE-MANAGERS.

An ANGLEPOISE or STANDARD LAMP with a strong beam, to light the screen from behind.

CARROT. A large cutout, with bites!

FLOWERS and VEGETABLES. If the children are not dressed up as these, they should hold cutouts in front of them.

COSTUMES

It would be simplest and very effective to use hats for the WITCHES and half-masks for the ANIMALS and INSECTS, and not to worry about complete costumes.

However, MEG and the other WITCHES could wear witches' dresses, and MEG's special shoes could be achieved with large painted cardboard buckles on black tap shoes. MOG could wear a black leotard with furry white stripes and tail. OWL, apart from a white feathery headdress, could wear a white 'puffball' dress.

The CUCKOO needs only a beak; this could be made of papier mâché, attached round the head with elastic.

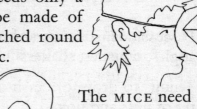

The MICE need only big ears and face-paint for whiskers. Tails would be a bonus!

The FROG, BEETLE, BAT and SPIDER could wear masks or headdresses, plus leotards. The FROG could be green, and the others basic black. It would be fun for the BAT to have wings and the SPIDER to have extra legs, which could hang down underneath his or her own arms.

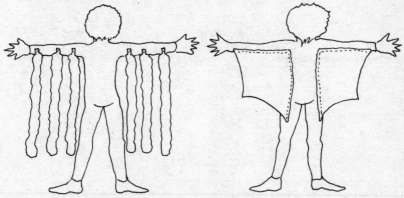

The STEGOSAURUS could be green with bright pink spots.

The STAGE-MANAGERS and PUPPETEERS would look best in jeans and dark T-shirts.

MUSIC AND SOUND EFFECTS

Percussion instruments, drums, xylophones, triangles, whistles, shakers

Things to drop for crash noises, e.g. tin trays, tin of nuts and bolts

LIGHTING

Apart from the shadow puppets, no special lighting is required

MEG AND THE STEGOSAURUS

STORYTELLER: Once upon a time there was a witch called Meg.
[MEG *enters and stands centre*]

She had a cat called Mog.
[MOG *enters and stands next to* MEG, *who strokes him*]

And an owl called Owl.
[OWL *enters and stands the other side of* MEG, *who strokes her*]

One night, they were in bed . . .
[*Two* STAGE-MANAGERS *bring on the cutout bed and hold it in front of* MEG, MOG *and* OWL. CUCKOO CLOCK *enters and stands next to the bed*]

. . . fast asleep.
[MEG, MOG *and* OWL *close their eyes and drop their heads*]

MEG: [*Snoring noise*]

OWL: Oooooooooo!

MEG: [*Snoring noise*]

OWL: Ooooooooo!

MEG: [*Snoring noise*]

OWL: Ooooooooo!

STORYTELLER: Time ticked by.

MUSICIANS: [*Tick-tocks on a xylophone*]

STORYTELLER: At midnight the cuckoo popped out of the clock.
[CUCKOO's *head appears through the clock or round the side*]

CUCKOO: Cuckoo! Cuckoo! Cuckoo! Cuckoo! Cuckoo! Cuckoo! Cuckoo! Cuckoo! Cuckoo! Cuckoo! Cuckoo! Cuckoo! Wake up!
[CUCKOO's *head goes back through the clock or round the side*]

[MEG, MOG *and* OWL *wake up and stretch*]

MEG: [*Yawns*]

MOG: Miaow!

OWL: Ooooo!

MEG: Time to get up!
[*The* STAGE-MANAGERS *take the bed off. The* CUCKOO CLOCK *follows*]

STORYTELLER: Meg, Mog and Owl went downstairs.

MUSICIANS: [*Rhythmic percussion*]
[MEG *leads* MOG *and* OWL, *in time with the music. They walk round twice in a circle as though going downstairs. Third time round* MEG *stops, suddenly*]

MEG: Here we are!
[MOG *bumps into* MEG. OWL *bumps into* MOG.]

MUSICIANS: [*Sound effects crash*]

MOG: Miaow!

OWL: Ooooo!

STORYTELLER: It was time for breakfast.

MEG Where's my cauldron?
[MOG *and* OWL *find it behind them*]

MOG: Miaow!

OWL: Ooooo!
[MEG, MOG *and* OWL *stand in a line by the cauldron*]

STORYTELLER Into the cauldron they put three eggs, a fish, some jam, a bottle of milk, a loaf of bread and a spoonful of cocoa.

[OWL *collects cutout ingredients from the props table and passes them to* MOG, *who passes them to* MEG, *who throws them in the cauldron, where they are received by a* STAGE-MANAGER, *crouching behind, who takes them behind the screen, out of the way of the waiting* STEGOSAURUS, *who now prepares to enter*]

Meg stirred it all up with her broomstick, and cast the magic spell.

[OWL *passes the broomstick to* MOG, *who passes it to* MEG, *who stirs with it*]

ALL: Abracadabra
Riddle-me-ree
By the power of my broomstick
Bring breakfast for three!

MUSICIANS: [*Magic notes on a triangle*]

STORYTELLER: But the spell went wrong!
[*From the cauldron, up pops a* STEGO-SAURUS]

MUSICIANS: [*Drumming sound*]

STEGOSAURUS: [*Growling noises*]
[MEG, MOG *and* OWL *back away*]

MEG: Aaaaah!

MOG: Miaow!

OWL: Ooooo!

MEG: You're not our breakfast!

STEGOSAURUS: No, you're *my* breakfast!

MEG: Aaaaah!

MOG: Miaow!

OWL: Ooooo!
[STEGOSAURUS *leaves the cauldron and chases* MEG, MOG *and* OWL *round and round*]

MUSICIANS: [*Chase music*]

STORYTELLER: It was a Stegosaurus!
[STEGOSAURUS *eventually goes.* MEG, MOG *and* OWL *look off after it*]

It went into the garden and started to eat Meg's flowers and vegetables.

STEGOSAURUS: [*Off – Chomping, yummy-yummy noises*]

MEG: Help!

MOG: Miaow!

OWL: Ooooo!

STORYTELLER: Meg, Mog and Owl flew off to find help.
[MEG *and* MOG *climb on the broomstick.* OWL *gets ready to fly*]

MUSICIANS [*Plus all*]: [*Whooshing noises*]
   [MEG, MOG *and* OWL *start to take off*]

   [STAGE-MANAGERS *bring on a screen and hold it ready. Behind it a light is turned on*]

   [PUPPETEERS *work the* MEG *and* MOG *and* OWL *puppets, flying them over the sky*]

   [*Flying music*]

STORYTELLER: Up in the sky they met the other witches. Tess . . .
   [*A* PUPPETEER *brings the* TESS *puppet to meet* MEG. *They circle*]

Jess . . .
   [*A* PUPPETEER *brings the* JESS *puppet to join them. They fly about*]

Bess . . .
   [*A* PUPPETEER *brings the* BESS *puppet to join them.*]

And Cress.
   [*A* PUPPETEER *brings the* CRESS *puppet to join them. They all fly about*]

Meg asked them to help her with a spell to get rid of the Stegosaurus. They all flew back to Meg's house.
   [*After a little more flying, the* MEG *and* MOG *and* OWL *puppets stop; the other* WITCHES

bump into them and all start to fall from the sky, till they disappear from the screen]

MUSICIANS: [*Descending whistle, followed by a loud crashing sound effect*]
[*The* PUPPETEERS *leave, followed by the* STAGE-MANAGERS *with the screen*]

[STEGOSAURUS *enters, fat, full and sleepy, carrying a large carrot*]

STORYTELLER: Meanwhile, the Stegosaurus had eaten most of Meg's flowers and vegetables, and was feeling very full and very sleepy.
[STEGOSAURUS *yawns and goes to sleep near the front*]

Meg, Mog and Owl, and Tess, Jess, Bess and Cress tiptoed in and prepared the Getting-rid-of-Stegosaurus spell.
[MEG, MOG, OWL *and the* WITCHES *enter and stand in a semicircle around* STEGO-SAURUS. *Then they get in a huddle, whispering about what to do. They all nod, and the* WITCHES *go to collect their ingredients*]

The witches each brought an ingredient for the spell. Tess brought a frog.
[TESS *leads in the* FROG. TESS *and* MEG *put the* FROG *into the cauldron*]

Jess brought a beetle.
[JESS *leads in the* BEETLE. JESS *and* MEG
put the BEETLE *into the cauldron*]

Bess brought a bat.
[BESS *leads in the* BAT. BESS *and* MEG *put
the* BAT *into the cauldron*]

And Cress brought a spider.
[CRESS *leads in the* SPIDER. CRESS *and*
MEG *put the* SPIDER *into the cauldron*]

Then they chanted their spell.
[*The four* WITCHES *go behind the cauldron
and wave their broomsticks.* MEG, MOG *and*
OWL *stay in front*]

ALL: Frog in a bog
Bat in a hat
Snap crackle pop
And fancy that!

MUSICIANS: [*Magic notes on a triangle*]

STORYTELLER: But the spell went wrong!

MUSICIANS: [*Percussion noises*]
[TESS, JESS, BESS *and* CRESS *start to wave
their arms and bodies and 'shrink' behind the
cauldron*]

TESS, JESS, BESS and CRESS: [*Scream*] Aaaaaaaaaah!
[*They disappear behind the screens*]

STORYTELLER: Tess, Jess, Bess and Cress turned into . . . mice!
[*Enter four* MICE *from behind the screens; they run round squeaking*]

MUSICIANS: [*Mouse-scuttling music*]

MICE: Ee! Ee! Ee! Ee!

MEG: Oh no!

MOG: Miaow!

OWL: Ooooo!
[MEG, MOG *and* OWL *watch as the* MICE *suddenly see* STEGOSAURUS]

MICE: [*Excited*] Ee! Ee! Ee! Ee!
[*They pounce on* STEGOSAURUS, *tickling and prodding.* STEGOSAURUS *wakes up*]

STEGOSAURUS: Aaaaaaaaaah!

STORYTELLER: The Stegosaurus was terrified of mice.

STEGOSAURUS: Aaaaaaaaaah!
[*The* MICE *chase off the terrified* STEGOSAURUS]

MUSICIANS: [*Chase music*]

STORYTELLER: It ran away as fast as its prehistoric legs would carry it, and never ever came back.

ALL: Hooray!

MEG: Maybe the spell didn't go wrong after
all!
[MOG *and* OWL *point towards the returning*
MICE]

MOG: Miaow!

OWL: Ooooo!

MEG: What? How do we change the mice
back to witches?
[MOG *and* OWL *nod*]

STORYTELLER: Meg decided to say the
'witches to mice' spell backwards!
[MEG *stands by the cauldron.* MOG *and* OWL
watch. The MICE *cluster in front*]

ALL: Bog a in frog
Hat a in bat
Pop crackle snap
That fancy and!

MUSICIANS: [*Magic notes*]
[*The* MICE *suddenly squeak and run round
the cauldron to behind the screens*]

MICE: Ee! Ee! Ee! Ee!
[*Then* TESS, JESS, BESS *and* CRESS *return
from behind the screens*]

MUSICIANS: [*Fanfare*]

MEG: It worked!

MOG: Miaow!

OWL: Ooooo!

ALL: Hooray!

STORYTELLER: Meg thanked the other witches for their help. But then Mog and Owl noticed that in the garden there were no flowers or vegetables at all.

MOG: [*Looking around, shaking his head*] Miaow!

OWL: [*Looking around, shaking her head*] Ooooo!

MEG: Stegosaurus ate the lot.

STORYTELLER: The witches had an idea.

TESS and JESS: We'll do a magic spell!

BESS and CRESS: To make the garden grow again!
[*All get into position.* MEG, MOG *and* OWL *are in the centre, with two* WITCHES *either side*]

STORYTELLER: Meg chanted the spell and the others said it after her.

MEG: Swallows and bluebells

ALL: Swallows and bluebells

MEG: And squawk of a crow

ALL: And squawk of a crow

MEG: Mix with a rainbow

ALL: Mix with a rainbow

MEG: To make the seeds grow!

ALL: To make the seeds grow!
    [*All look around, hopefully. Nothing happens*]

MEG: [*To audience*] Please. *All* join in!

    Swallows and bluebells

ALL [*And audience*]: Swallows and bluebells

MEG: And squawk of a crow

ALL [*And audience*]: And squawk of a crow

MEG: Mix with a rainbow

ALL [*And audience*]: Mix with a rainbow

MEG: To make the seeds grow!

ALL [*And audience*]: To make the seeds grow!

MUSICIANS: [*Growing sounds, percussion*]
    [*Enter as many* FLOWERS *and* VEGETABLES
    *as possible (children carrying cutouts, or dressed
    in costume)*]

    [*When all have arrived . . .*]

STORYTELLER: The garden was full of flowers and vegetables again. Meg thanked the witches for their help and they flew up and away, into the sky.

MUSICIANS: [*Whooshing noises*]
[TESS, JESS, BESS *and* CRESS *leave, astride their broomsticks*]

STORYTELLER: Meg, Mog and Owl were tired after their busy night. So they went back to bed.
[STAGE-MANAGERS *bring on the bed cutout, and place it amongst the* FLOWERS *and* VEGETABLES. MEG, MOG *and* OWL *stand behind it*]

One by one they fell fast asleep.

Owl . . .

OWL: Ooooo!
[OWL *goes to sleep*]

STORYTELLER: Mog . . .

MOG: Miaow!
[MOG *goes to sleep*]

STORYTELLER: And Meg . . .

MEG: [*Yawns*]
[MEG *goes to sleep*]

STORYTELLER: The end.

MEG AND SIR GEORGE

THE PEOPLE IN THE PLAY

STAGE-MANAGERS, who carry on the cutout scenery and hold it during the scenes

MUSICIANS/SOUND-EFFECTS MAKERS, with various keyboards, percussion instruments, coconut shells for horses' hoofs, wood blocks and xylophones. A teacher might play the waltz tune and the dance music at the end on a piano or keyboard

STORYTELLER. Probably an adult, or several children dividing the lines between them

MEG, the witch

MOG, Meg's cat

OWL, Meg's owl

SIR GEORGE, a peace-loving knight. Speaking with a lisp might add humour

GHOST I

GHOST 2

SPECTATORS at the jousting match. As many as possible

SIR FRANÇOIS, a pompous, war-loving knight

SCENERY AND PROPS

A similar layout to that suggested for *Meg and the Stegosaurus*. Instead of screens, two towers suggesting castle battlements could be used.

No cauldron is necessary in this play.

The TABLE and FOUR-POSTER BED are cut-outs.

MEG'S BROOMSTICK.

HOBBYHORSES for SIR GEORGE and SIR FRAN-ÇOIS. These could be adapted from toy hobby-horses, or special ones could be made on braces to wear round the waist. SIR GEORGE's should be red and white; SIR FRANÇOIS's should be green and black.

LANCES. These can be made of foam rubber attached to broom handles.

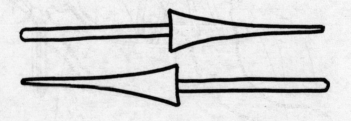

If a MAYPOLE is used, it should be held by two STAGE-MANAGERS to give stability.

COSTUMES

MEG, MOG and OWL as in *Meg and the Stegosaurus*.

GHOSTS should wear white material with eye holes. Old sheets could be adapted to fit.

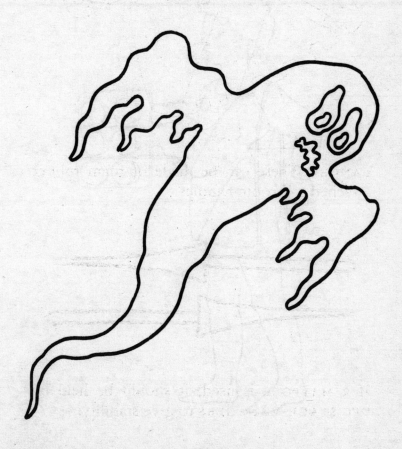

SIR GEORGE and SIR FRANÇOIS should wear funny armour (possibly made with kitchen utensils) over basic tunics. SIR GEORGE wears his armour only for the jousting match.

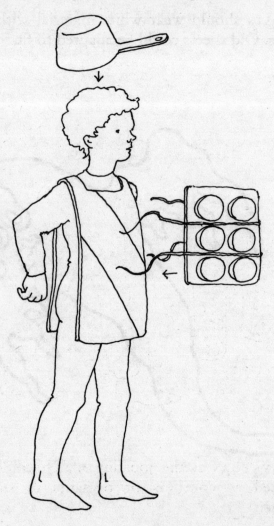

SPECTATORS at the jousting match could be dressed as courtiers or peasants in simple tunics.

MUSIC AND SOUND EFFECTS

In this play there is much scope for improvised
music and sound effects. It is true that a piano
could most easily play chase music or a jaunty
waltz, but all the other effects can be created
with an array of everyday objects: cutlery, tin
plates, drinking mugs, a tin tray to make a
crash, coconut shells, clanking chains and various whistles and blowers. The sound of a
door creaking can be made effectively by twist-
ing a balloon between the hands. Instead of a
xylophone to suggest time ticking by, two
bottles filled to different levels with water
would work well. The fanfares would be funni-
est performed on toy trumpets.

LIGHTING

No special lighting is required, but it might be
effective to lower the lights for the night-time
ghost scene.

MEG AND SIR GEORGE

STORYTELLER: Once upon a time there was a witch called Meg.
[MEG *enters and stands centre*]

She had a cat called Mog.
[MOG *enters and stands next to* MEG, *who strokes him*]

And an owl called Owl.
[OWL *enters and stands the other side of* MEG, *who strokes her*]

They went to stay in a castle.
[MEG, MOG *and* OWL *look pleased and excitedly look around, moving left of centre*]

MUSICIANS: [*A short fanfare*]
[*Enter* SIR GEORGE *from behind a tower screen. He greets his guests*]

SIR GEORGE: Welcome to my castle. I am Sir George.

MEG: [*With a curtsy*] Hallo, Sir George.

MOG: [*With a bow*] Miaow!

OWL: [*With a flutter*] Oo oo!

SIR GEORGE: You must be exhausted after your journey. Come share some supper with me.

> [MEG *puts down her broomstick at the front as two* STAGE-MANAGERS *bring on the cutout table. They hold it in front of* SIR GEORGE, MEG, MOG *and* OWL, *who mime eating and drinking*]

MUSICIANS [*And others*]: [*Eating noises: cutlery on tin plates, clinking of goblets*]

STORYTELLER: After a delicious meal, Sir George suddenly burst into tears.

SIR GEORGE: [*Big weeping and sobbing*]

MEG: What's the matter?

SIR GEORGE: Alas! Sir François, the knight who liveth in yon castle next door, hath challenged me to a jousting match – tomorrow.

MOG: Miaow!

OWL: Ooooo!

MEG: A jousting match. That'll be fun.

SIR GEORGE: For me 'twill be no fun. If I lose, he winneth my castle. [*More weeping*]

MEG: You might er . . . winneth.

SIR GEORGE: Not against Sir François. *Nobody* winneth against him. He is enormous strong and he loveth fighting. I hate fighting. [*More weeping*]

STORYTELLER: It was bedtime.
    [*The* STAGE-MANAGERS *take the table off*]

Sir George showed his guests to their room.
    [SIR GEORGE *mimes to* MEG, MOG *and* OWL *to follow him*]

They climbed up the spiral stairs.

MUSICIANS: [*Rhythmic percussion*]
    [SIR GEORGE *leads* MEG, MOG *and* OWL *in time with the music. They walk round and round in a circle as though going upstairs. After six small circles,* SIR GEORGE *stops suddenly*]

SIR GEORGE: Here we are!
    [MEG *bumps into* SIR GEORGE. MOG *bumps into* MEG. OWL *bumps into* MOG]

MUSICIANS: [*Sound effects crash*]

MEG: Aaaaah!

MOG: Miaow!

OWL: Ooooo!

SIR GEORGE: Good night. Take no notice of the ghost.

[SIR GEORGE *exits quickly*]

OWL: Ooooo!

MOG: Miaow!

MEG: Ghost? He must have been joking. There are no such things as ghosts.

[MOG *and* OWL *cuddle up to* MEG *for protection*]

STORYTELLER: They climbed into a four-poster bed . . .

[*Two* STAGE-MANAGERS *bring on the cutout bed and hold it centre.* MEG, MOG *and* OWL *mime climbing into it, and stand behind it*]

. . . and went to sleep.

[MEG, MOG *and* OWL *close their eyes and drop their heads*]

MEG: [*Snoring noise*]

OWL: Ooooooooo!

MEG: [*Snoring noise*]

OWL: Ooooooooo!

MEG: [*Snoring noise*]

OWL: Ooooooooo!

STORYTELLER: Time ticked by.

MUSICIANS: [*Tick-tocks on xylophone*]

STORYTELLER: In the dead of night, Meg, Mog and Owl heard weird noises.

MUSICIANS: [*A spooky door-creaking sound*]
[OWL *slowly wakes up and looks frightened*]

[*A spooky chain-clanking sound*]
[MOG *wakes up and looks frightened*]

[*A spooky moan*]
[MEG *wakes up and looks frightened*]

[*Door creak, chain clank and moan all together*]
[MEG, MOG *and* OWL *all react*]

MEG: Aaaaah!

MOG: Miaow!

OWL: Ooooo!
[*Silence*]

MEG: This is silly. Let's go back to sleep.
[MEG, MOG *and* OWL *close their eyes and drop their heads again*]

[*Snoring noise*]

OWL: Oooooooooo!

MEG: [*Snoring noise*]

OWL: Oooooooooo!

MEG: [*Snoring noise*]

OWL: Ooooooooooo!

MUSICIANS: [*Spooky rumble on a drum or keyboard*]
[*Enter a* GHOST *from behind a tower screen. It taps* OWL *on the shoulder, then looms over her*]

[OWL *wakes, sees the* GHOST, *reacts and is chased behind the tower screen by the* GHOST]

OWL: Ooooo!
[MEG *and* MOG *are still asleep*]

MUSICIANS: [*Spooky rumble*]
[*A* GHOST *enters from behind the other tower screen, taps* MOG *on the shoulder, then looms over him*]

[MOG *wakes, sees the* GHOST, *reacts and is chased behind the tower screen by the* GHOST]

MOG: Miaow!
[MEG *is still asleep*]

MUSICIANS: [*Spooky rumble*]
[*The* GHOSTS *return and climb into bed either side of* MEG. *They tap her on each shoulder*]

MEG: [*Sleepily*] It's all right, Mog. It's all right, Owl. Go to sleep.
[*She puts her arms round the* GHOSTS]

GHOSTS: Woooooaaaaahhhhh!
[MEG *wakes and sees the* GHOSTS]

MEG: Aaaaaaaaaah!
[*She runs round the bed, picks up her broomstick, and stands centre*]

[*The* GHOSTS *very slowly start to advance towards her*]

STORYTELLER: Meg cast a magic spell.

MEG: Hocus-pocus
Dear oh dear
Ghastly ghosts
Please disappear!

MUSICIANS: [*Magic notes*]
[*The* GHOSTS *suddenly dash off, one behind each tower screen*]

[MEG *looks round*]

MEG: It worked!

STORYTELLER: Meg went back to bed.
[MEG *puts down her broomstick in front, then goes back behind the bed*]

But Mog and Owl had disappeared!

MEG: [*Searching*] Mog! Owl!

MUSICIANS: [*Spooky rumble*]
[*Two* GHOSTS *enter, one from behind each tower screen. In fact, these* GHOSTS *are* MOG *and* OWL, *in* GHOST *costumes, but* MEG *doesn't know that. Hopefully, the audience doesn't know that either yet!*]

[*Suddenly* MEG *sees the* GHOSTS]

MEG: Aaaaah! The spell didn't work after all!
[*The* GHOSTS *chase* MEG *all over the place*]

MUSICIANS: [*Chase music*]
[MEG *eventually stops, terrified*]

[*The two* GHOSTS *suddenly lift off their* GHOST *costumes and throw them over* MEG, *who struggles with them for a while, then sees* MOG *and* OWL *standing revealed, laughing at her*]

MEG: It was you two all the time! I told you there were no such things as ghosts!

MUSICIANS: [*Long, noisy fanfare to announce the start of the jousting match*]
[MOG *and* OWL *mime to* MEG *that* they *saw real* GHOSTS, *as all three exit behind the tower screens, taking the* GHOST *costumes with them*]

[*The* STAGE-MANAGERS *take off the bed*]

[*As the fanfare ends,* SIR GEORGE, *on his hobbyhorse and carrying his lance, enters nervously, ending up to one side*]

MUSICIANS: [*Horse hoofs*]

STORYTELLER: Next day Sir George prepared for the jousting match. He was very nervous.
[SIR GEORGE *trembles*]

MUSICIANS: [*Trembling sounds on wood blocks*]

STORYTELLER: The spectators arrived.

MUSICIANS: [*Busy music*]
[*The* SPECTATORS *enter and stand in rows at the back.* MEG, MOG *and* OWL *enter with them*]

MEG: Good luck, Sir George!

SIR GEORGE: Thanks. 'Twill be necessary, methinks. Sir François is tough as a tree trunk and strong as an ox.

MUSICIANS: [*Horse hoofs approaching*]

STORYTELLER: Sir François made his entrance.
[SIR FRANÇOIS *enters impressively on his hobbyhorse and carrying his lance. He goes to one side, opposite* SIR GEORGE]

MUSICIANS: [*Short fanfare*]

SPECTATORS: Boooo!

SIR FRANÇOIS: Art thou ready, Sir George?

SIR GEORGE: Aye, Sir François. As ready as I'll ever be.

SIR FRANÇOIS: We joust thrice. Two falls, a submission or a knockout to decide.

SIR GEORGE: If thou sayest so.

MUSICIANS: [*Fanfare and horse hoofs*]
[SIR GEORGE *and* SIR FRANÇOIS *meet in the middle and 'present lances', then exit either side*]

[*The* SPECTATORS *look off expectantly*]

[*Horse hoofs approaching and drum rumble*]
[SIR GEORGE *enters slowly, hiding his eyes in fear*]

[SIR FRANÇOIS *enters confidently. He has only to gently prod* SIR GEORGE *to make him fall*]

SIR FRANÇOIS: Ha ha ha. One love!

SPECTATORS: Boooo!
[SIR FRANÇOIS *exits the side opposite the one from which he entered*]

[MEG, MOG *and* OWL *come forward and help* SIR GEORGE *to stand. He exits the other side*]

MOG: Miaow!
[*He mimes that they should help*]

MEG: What? We should help?

MOG: Miaow.

MEG: But how?
[MOG *has a sudden idea and picks up the broomstick lying at the front. He hands it to* MEG, *then jumps over it*]

Jump the broomstick! Good idea!
[*She stands centre, holding out the broomstick*]

MUSICIANS: [*Horse hoofs approaching and drum roll*]
[SIR FRANÇOIS *enters. He cannot see the broomstick, but his horse can and rears up, then backs a little*]

[*Whinnies*]
[SIR FRANÇOIS *tries again. The horse rears up again*]

[*Whinnies, then horse hoofs approaching and drum roll*]
[SIR GEORGE *enters, hiding his eyes in fear, but with lance outstretched. His lance happens*

to hit the tottering SIR FRANÇOIS, *who falls*]

SIR GEORGE: [*Amazed*] One all!

SPECTATORS: Hooray! Hooray!
   [SIR FRANÇOIS *staggers up and both* KNIGHTS *exit*]

MEG: [*Calling to* SIR GEORGE *as he exits*] One more fall to win, Sir George!

OWL: [*Coming forward, miming 'a magic spell'*] Whoo! Whoo!

MEG: What? Make a magic spell? What if it goes wrong?

OWL: [*Urgently*] Whoo! Whoo!

MUSICIANS: [*Drum roll*]

MEG: All right then.
   [*She waves her broomstick*]

Give poor Sir George
A better chance
Make Sir François
Drop his lance!
   [*She goes back to the* SPECTATORS]

MUSICIANS: [*Horse hoofs approaching and drum roll*]
   [*Both* KNIGHTS *enter*]

[*Suddenly* SIR FRANÇOIS *stops dead, as though magically hypnotized*]

[*A jaunty waltz tune*]
[SIR FRANÇOIS *and his horse start dancing in time with the music. He cannot control himself and spins round, confused*]

[SIR GEORGE *stops and watches in amazement*]

SPECTATORS: [*Laughter*]

MEG: [*Stepping forward and looking up*] I said 'drop his lance', not 'stop and dance'! Oh dear!

[*The music gets faster.* SIR FRANÇOIS *revolves giddily. Suddenly he drops his lance, and falls over*]

MEG: [*Pointing to the lance*] It worked after all!

SIR FRANÇOIS: I submit! Sir George is the winner!

SPECTATORS: Hooray! Hooray!

MUSICIANS: [*Triumphant fanfare*]
[SIR FRANÇOIS *beats an ignominious retreat and exits*]

[SIR GEORGE, *delighted, rushes to* MEG]

SIR GEORGE: Thank you! Thank you! My castle is saved!

SPECTATORS: Hooray! Hooray!

STORYTELLER: And everybody joined in the celebration – except Sir François!

MUSICIANS: [*A happy dance*]
[*Everyone dances; if possible, round a maypole*]

THE END

MEG ON THE MOON

THE PEOPLE IN THE PLAY

STAGE-MANAGERS, who carry on the cutout scenery and hold it during the scenes

MUSICIANS/SOUND-EFFECTS MAKERS

VOICES. A speaking choir. Alternatively all the other members of the cast could speak their words

PUPPETEERS to carry cutout puppets or poles representing moon, stars and other heavenly bodies

STORYTELLER. Probably an adult, or several children dividing the lines between them

MEG, the witch

MOG, Meg's cat

OWL, Meg's owl

ASTRONAUTS. As few as two or as many as six

SCENERY AND PROPS

The acting area is similar to that recommended for *Meg and the Stegosaurus*, but it may be advisable to use the screens further downstage as wing flats. This will enable STAGE-MANAGERS, PUPPETEERS and cast to enter from and exit behind them.

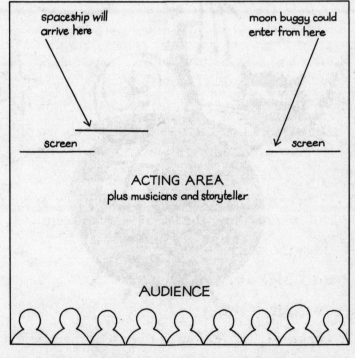

The CAULDRON is the same as for *Meg and the Stegosaurus*.

MEG'S BROOMSTICK.

Cutout PUPPETS on poles – moon, stars, rockets, heavenly bodies, cauldron (with MEG, MOG and OWL inside), spaceship (with string joining it to the cauldron).

The MOON BUGGY is a cutout, behind which MEG, MOG and OWL can stand and carry it when moving.

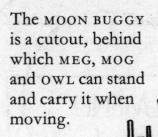

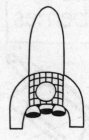

The SPACESHIP is also a cutout. When placed alongside the screen, it allows the ASTRONAUTS to enter and exit behind it.

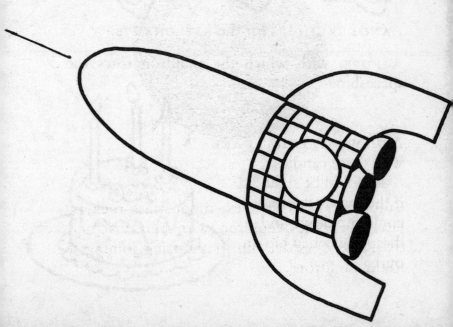

A BOARD made of thin card. On one side is written Hi!, on the other a menu, as illustrated.

Three identical cutout FOODPACKS.

HANDKERCHIEFS for the ASTRONAUTS.

A ROPE, with which the cauldron tows the spaceship.

A cutout BIRTHDAY CAKE with three candles.
It would be splendid if the candle flames could flip down and disappear when blown out!

COSTUMES

MEG, MOG and OWL, PUPPETEERS and STAGE-MANAGERS as described in *Meg and the Stegosaurus*.

The ASTRONAUTS could wear boiler suits or track suits, and motor-cycle helmets with visors (or similar). Large 'moon' boots would look good, too.

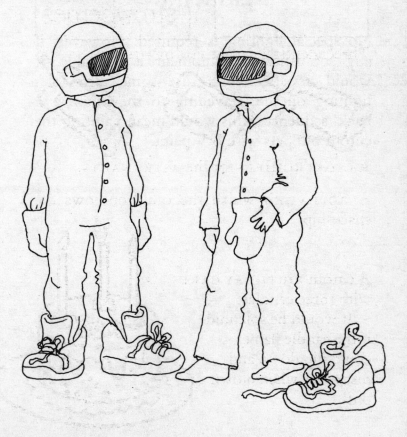

MUSIC AND SOUND EFFECTS

Percussion instruments, drums, xylophones and others to make 'moon music', whooshes, a splash and other noises. Some can be vocalized! A teacher might play an electronic keyboard for the 'travelling back to earth' scene.

LIGHTING

No special lighting is required. However, if any sophisticated equipment is available, it would be effective to use some ultraviolet lighting on the 'travelling to the moon and back' sequences; this would mean painting the cutout puppets with UV paint.

MEG ON THE MOON

STORYTELLER: This is a story about a witch
called Meg . . .
[MEG *enters, with her broomstick, and stands
centre*]

. . . her cat, Mog . . .
[MOG *enters and stands next to* MEG, *who
strokes him*]

. . . and her owl, Owl.
[OWL *enters and stands the other side of* MEG,
who strokes her]

It was Mog's birthday. For his birthday
treat, Mog wanted to fly to the moon.
[MOG *takes* MEG's *broomstick and mimes
flying on it*]

MOG: Miaow!

MEG: On my broomstick? I don't think the
broomstick would carry us that far.
[MOG *hands* MEG *her broomstick, then mimes
a spaceship taking off*]

MEG: A spaceship? We haven't got a spaceship.

MOG: [*Sad*] Miaow.

OWL: [*Suddenly*] Oooooh!

STORYTELLER: Owl had an idea.
[OWL *and* MOG *fetch the cutout cauldron and
place it centre in front of* MEG. *They join her
behind it*]

Use Meg's cauldron as a spaceship.

MUSICIANS: [*Magic-spell music*]

MEG: [*Waving her broomstick*]
Cauldron, carry us up high
Like a spaceship in the sky
To the moon by magic spell
Stand by for countdown, earth, farewell!

ALL [*Including the audience*]: Ten, nine, eight,
seven, six, five, four, three, two, one –
LIFT-OFF!

MUSICIANS and VOICES: [*Take-off noises,
whooshes, ascending notes on a xylophone or
keyboard*]
[MEG, MOG *and* OWL *look excited, as though
they are taking off*]

[*During the following poem,* PUPPETEERS
carrying cutouts on poles of the moon, stars,

*rockets and heavenly bodies enter and move
round the cauldron, as though the cauldron is
passing them in space.* MEG, MOG *and* OWL
excitedly look up at them]

VOICES: [*Individual lines or all together*]
Meg and Mog and Owl are flying to the
  moon
See it on the skyline hanging like a big
  balloon
Up among the stars
The Milky Way and Mars
Meg and Mog and Owl on a day trip to the
  moon
Away, away on a
Day trip to the moon.

Operation moonquest, supersonic flight
Climbing in a cauldron quicker than the
  speed of light
Up and up they race
Way out in outer space
Meg and Mog and Owl on a day trip to the
  moon
Away, away on a
Day trip to the moon.

Looking at the lunar landscape drawing
  near
Standing by for landing, Meg and Mog and
  Owl are here

Time to go sightseeing
Then fly home for tea
Meg and Mog and Owl on a day trip to the
      moon
Away, away on a
Day trip to the moon.
    [*The* PUPPETEERS *have exited during the last
    verse*]

MUSICIANS and VOICES: [*Moon music – electronic bleeps on a keyboard and vocalized 'blip
blop' noises*]
    [MEG, MOG *and* OWL *climb from the caul-
    dron*]

STORYTELLER: Meg, Mog and Owl found it
strange walking on the moon. They felt
very light.
    [MEG, MOG *and* OWL *walk around doing
    slow-motion 'moon-walking'. Maybe* MOG *rolls
    on the ground in cat-like fashion, but very
    slowly!*]

    [*After a while . . .*]

They collected some moondust. Meg
thought it might be useful for a magic spell.
    [MEG *sees the moondust.* MOG *takes her broom-
    stick,* OWL *takes her hat. They mime sweeping
    moondust into the hat, still in slow motion!*]

    [MEG *carefully puts on her hat again*]

[MEG, MOG *and* OWL *walk towards one side of the acting area*]

STORYTELLER: Suddenly they saw . . .
[MEG, MOG *and* OWL *point behind the screen*]

MEG: [*Slow, like a record played at the wrong speed*] Loo-ook!

MOG: [*Slow*] Mia-o-w!

OWL: [*Slow*] Oo-oo-ooh!
[*Two* STAGE-MANAGERS *bring on the cut-out moon buggy and put it in front of* MEG, MOG *and* OWL, *who look as though they are ready to drive off. The* STAGE-MANAGERS *exit*]

STORYTELLER: . . . a moon buggy. They went for a ride.

MUSICIANS and VOICES: [*Slow-speed-revving-engine noises; moon noises continue 'under'*]
[MEG, MOG *and* OWL *set off, crossing towards the other side of the acting area in the moon buggy, carrying the cutout themselves*]

[*At the same time, a* STAGE-MANAGER *enters and, in slow motion, takes off the cauldron, as though* MEG, MOG *and* OWL *are driving away from it. The cauldron disappears behind a screen*]

[*Perhaps* MEG *pulls a lever, making the moon*

buggy go backwards a little way, then corrects it and the journey continues]

[*As they reach the other side . . .*]

STORYTELLER: Suddenly they saw . . .

MEG: [*Slow*] Loo-ook!

MOG: [*Slow*] Mia-o-w!

OWL: [*Slow*] Oo-oo-ooh!
[*Two* STAGE-MANAGERS *bring on a cutout spaceship and hold it alongside the screen*]

STORYTELLER: . . . a spaceship.
[MEG, MOG *and* OWL *have driven the moon buggy past the spaceship. Now they 'park' it, or* STAGE-MANAGERS *remove it*]

[MEG, MOG *and* OWL *approach the spaceship, in slow motion.* MOG *knocks three times on the side — big, slow knocks*]

MUSICIANS: [*Knocks, on a xylophone or keyboard; moon noises continue 'under'*]

STORYTELLER: Out came astronauts.
[*As* MEG *and* MOG *back away,* ASTRO-NAUTS *come out of the spaceship. All moon-walk. The last* ASTRONAUT *holds up a cardboard message saying: Hi!*]

[*All the* ASTRONAUTS *wave*]

[MEG, MOG *and* OWL *wave back*]

VOICES: Are you . . .
[ASTRONAUTS *point to* MEG, MOG *and* OWL]

. . . hungry?
[ASTRONAUTS *rub their tummies, then open their arms in a questioning way*]

STORYTELLER: . . . asked the astronauts.

We are . . .
[MEG, MOG *and* OWL *nod*]

. . . hungry . . .
[MEG, MOG *and* OWL *rub their tummies*]

. . . replied Meg, Mog and Owl. The astronauts asked them what they would like to eat.
[*The last* ASTRONAUT *turns over his cardboard message. It reads: Menu – hamburger, fish fingers, strawberries. The* ASTRONAUT *walks to* MEG, MOG *and* OWL, *who point to their favourite meal*]

Owl fancied hamburger.
[OWL *points to 'hamburger'*]

Mog wanted fish fingers.
[MOG *points to 'fish fingers'*]

Meg asked for strawberries.
[MEG *points to 'strawberries'*]

[*The* ASTRONAUT *signals to the other* ASTRO-
NAUTS; *the one nearest the spaceship reaches
behind it and produces, one at a time (handed
to him by a* STAGE-MANAGER), *three identical foodpacks with straws. These are passed
down the line to* MEG, MOG *and* OWL (*all in
slow motion!*), *who look at them in surprise,
but then try sucking the straws and enjoy the
taste of the contents*]

MUSICIANS and VOICES: [*Slurping, sucking noises*]
[MEG, MOG *and* OWL *pass the foodpacks to
the nearest* ASTRONAUT]

STORYTELLER: Meg, Mog and Owl said thank
you and started to wave goodbye.
[MEG, MOG *and* OWL *wave*]

But the astronauts said . . .
[*The* ASTRONAUTS *point to the spaceship*]

VOICES: [*Slow speed*] Our spaceship has broken
down. Please help us!
[MEG *mimes having an idea.* MOG *holds her
broomstick, while from her hat she mimes
taking some moondust*]

STORYTELLER: Meg cast a magic spell.

MEG: [*Slow speed*]
Magic moondust
Through the sky
Make the astronauts
All fly!

STORYTELLER: But the spell went wrong.
[*The* ASTRONAUTS *produce handkerchiefs and dab their space helmets (they cannot reach their eyes!)*]

VOICES: [*Slow speed*] Boo hoo! Boo hoo! [*And other crying noises*]

MEG: [*Slow speed*] Oh dear! I said 'make them fly', not 'make them *cry*'!

STORYTELLER: Mog and Owl had an idea.
[MOG *and* OWL *huddle together, then look up*]

OWL: [*Slow speed*] Oo-oo-ooh!

MOG: [*Slow speed*] Mia-o-w!
[MOG, *giving* MEG *back her broomstick, mimes pulling*]

STORYTELLER: They suggested towing the spaceship back to earth. The astronauts agreed.

MUSICIANS: [*Moon music for the preparations*]
[*The* ASTRONAUTS *return to the spaceship and go behind it, as though going inside*]

[*Meanwhile,* MOG *and* OWL *fetch the cauldron from where the* STAGE-MANAGER *left it behind the screen. They place it near this screen and stand behind it*]

[MEG *collects one end of a rope from the last* ASTRONAUT *to enter the spaceship, and takes it to the cauldron.* MOG *takes the rope and pulls it taut*]

MEG: [*Waving her broomstick*]
Cauldron, quickly as you can
Take us back where we began
To the earth by magic spell
Stand by for countdown, moon, farewell!

ALL [*Including the audience*]: Ten, nine, eight, seven, six, five, four, three, two, one – LIFT-OFF!

MUSICIANS and VOICES: [*Take-off noises, whooshes, ascending notes on a xylophone or keyboard*]
[MEG, MOG *and* OWL *carry the cauldron off behind the screen, pulling the spaceship, which, carried from behind by a* STAGE-MANAGER, *tips over a little and exits behind the screen*]

STORYTELLER: Cauldron and spaceship headed back to earth.

MUSICIANS: [*Travelling-through-space music*]
[PUPPETEERS *carrying cutouts on poles*

*act out the flight. The cauldron tows the space-
ship past stars, rockets and heavenly bodies.
The moon cutout also appears, then recedes*]

[*Eventually all the* PUPPETEERS *exit*]

STORYTELLER: At last the cauldron and the
spaceship landed . . . in Meg's pond.

MUSICIANS: [*Big splashing noises*]

STORYTELLER: Meg invited the astronauts to
Mog's birthday tea.
[MEG, *carrying a cutout birthday cake, leads
on* MOG, OWL *and the* ASTRONAUTS]

ALL: [*Singing*] Happy birthday to you
             Happy birthday to you
             Happy birthday, dear Mog
             Happy birthday to you.
[MOG *mimes blowing out the candles on the cake*]

Hooray!

STORYTELLER: The end.

MEG AT THE ZOO

THE PEOPLE IN THE PLAY

STAGE-MANAGERS, who carry on the cutout scenery and hold it during the scenes. They could be dressed as zookeepers

MUSICIANS/SOUND-EFFECTS MAKERS, with various percussion instruments and keyboards or piano

STORYTELLER. An adult or child, or several children dividing the lines between them

MEG, the witch

MOG, Meg's cat

OWL, Meg's owl

ANIMALS IN THE ZOO. As many and as varied as will fit in the acting area! Each animal (or pair of animals if preferred) is introduced, enters, utters an appropriate animal call, then goes to a cage upstage to witness the rest of the play

ELEPHANT. The actor is never seen! But he or she makes loud trumpeting noises offstage and manipulates the elephant's trunk which appears round a screen.

ZOOKEEPER

TIGER

SCENERY AND PROPS

The staging of this play would be helped by proper 'wings'. These can be created by extra screens downstage.

The MUSICIANS should not be in the acting area, but to one side by the audience.

MEG'S BROOMSTICK.

Cutout CAGES with bars (not too close to-gether), to stretch across the upstage area. These could be made out of cardboard. They need not be self-standing. An alternative idea is to use a number of cardboard cage-bars only. These can be held by the ANIMALS.

A cutout CAGE DOOR (TIGER's cage), with a key and lock painted on.

SCRUBBING BRUSH (for zookeeper).

ELEPHANT'S TRUNK. This could be made from a long coiled spring, or a tube of material stuffed with old tights! It needs to bend enough to be swung from behind the screen around the ZOOKEEPER's body. A STAGE-MANAGER should 'wear' the trunk like an extended sleeve and, standing on a stool behind the screen, swing the arm out, making the trunk catch the ZOOKEEPER.

ZOOKEEPER'S SPECTACLES. Heavy-rimmed. Once the ELEPHANT (offstage) has sat on them, another pair should be used, broken into three pieces. For convenience these should be attached to each other with thread.

'FEATHER OF RAVEN'. A real feather or quill.

'LEG OF A FROG'. Part of a rubber 'joke' frog.

FOOD BUCKET
marked 'Tiger'.

TIGER'S TOOTH.
Cutout or papier mâché,
larger than a real one!

**ELEVEN-PENCE
COIN.** Or a ten pence
and a one pence!

MAGIC HANDKERCHIEF, to make the spec-
tacle pieces disappear. This is in fact two
handkerchiefs sewn together, leaving one sec-
tion open. The corner nearest the opening
should have a small bead
or button sewn to it, for
easy identification. The use
of the magic handkerchief
is described in the play.

secret
pocket

COSTUMES

MEG, MOG and OWL as in *Meg and the Stego-saurus*. Meg's cloak needs a pocket.

The ANIMALS at the zoo can be as simple or as fanciful as desired, using masks, headdresses, tails, wings and other appropriate appendages.

The ZOOKEEPER needs wellington boots, a peaked cap and an apron.

The TIGER should wear a stripy costume, maybe made from a tight-fitting boiler suit or 'combinations', boots and a sola topi. A moustache could be effective. And a tail!

MUSIC AND SOUND EFFECTS

Percussion instruments, drums, xylophones, triangles, whistles, shakers. Things to drop for
crash noises. A keyboard would be useful for
chase music.

LIGHTING

No special lighting is necessary, but it would
be useful to be able to create a blackout by
turning all the lights off.

MEG AT THE ZOO

STORYTELLER: This is a story about a witch called Meg . . .

[MEG *enters, with her broomstick, and stands centre*]

. . . and her cat, Mog . . .

[MOG *enters and stands next to* MEG, *who strokes him*]

. . . and her owl, Owl.

[OWL *enters and stands the other side of* MEG, *who strokes her*]

Meg had been checking through her magic spell ingredients.

MEG: I've got plenty of dried spiders and lizards' livers, but I haven't got one tiger's tooth.

OWL: Whooooo?

MEG: Tooth of a tiger. A very powerful ingredient.

MOG: [*Having an idea*] Miaow!
      [*He mimes flying*]

MEG: What? Go and find one?

MOG: [*Nodding*] Miaow.

MEG: Good idea. Where? Where could we find
      a tiger?

OWL: [*After a thinking pause*] Zooooo! Zooooo!

MEG: A zoo! Of course. Come on! All aboard!
      [MEG *and* MOG *put their legs astride the
      broomstick.* OWL *gets ready to fly too*]

      [MEG *concentrates*]

MUSICIANS: [*Magic spell notes*]

MEG: Broomstick, fly
      Up in the sky
      Speed us to
      The nearest zoo!

MUSICIANS: [*Whoosh take-off noises*]
      [MEG, MOG *and* OWL '*rev up*', *then exit, as
      though taking off*]

STORYTELLER: At the zoo, for all the animals
      it was a normal day.

MUSICIANS: [*Music to introduce the* ANIMALS]
      [*The* STORYTELLER *introduces each* ANIMAL.

*(As many as required; the following are sugges-
tions. Different animals, or more or less animals, can be used, but no elephant and no
tiger, for reasons which will become apparent!)]*

[Each ANIMAL *enters, stands centre, makes
its animal call, then goes and waits upstage]*

STORYTELLER: The monkey.
            The lion.
            The penguin.
            The snake.
            The tortoise.
            The bear.
            The vulture.
            The kangaroo.
            The moose.
            The panda.
            The anteater.
            The zebra.

[When all the ANIMALS *have been introduced,*
STAGE-MANAGERS *bring on cutout cages and
stand them in front of the* ANIMALS, *who hold
them up]*

[A STAGE-MANAGER *brings on a cage door
and holds it next to the back screen onstage left]*

MUSICIANS: *[A high-pitched electronic sound]*

STORYTELLER: Suddenly the animals heard a
strange sound in the sky.
       [The ANIMALS *look up]*

STORYTELLER: They saw Meg, Mog and Owl circling.
[*The* ANIMALS *look round in a circle, as though following the flight of* MEG, MOG *and* OWL. *Their eyes end up looking offstage right*]

They saw them land.

MUSICIANS: [*Descending electronic sound, followed by huge crash, bang, tinkle-tinkle*]
[*The* ANIMALS *hide their eyes, then open them as* MEG, MOG *and* OWL *enter*]

MEG: Now. Tiger hunt. Mog, you go that way [*Pointing right*]. Owl, you go that way [*Pointing left*]. And good luck.
[MOG *and* OWL *exit*]

[MEG *starts looking at the* ANIMALS *in the cages upstage*]

[*Suddenly she hears a noise from offstage right. She looks off*]

ELEPHANT: [*Voice off*] [*Loud trumpeting*]

ZOOKEEPER: [*Voice off*] Now stand still, there's a good girl.

ELEPHANT: [*Off*] [*Trumpeting*]

ZOOKEEPER: [*Off*] Stand *still*!

MEG: [*Calling*] Excuse me.

ELEPHANT: [*Off*] [*Trumpeting*]

ZOOKEEPER: [*Off*] You're asking for trouble, you know. Big trouble.

ELEPHANT: [*Off*] [*Trumpeting*]

ZOOKEEPER: [*Off*] Now don't be silly. Put me down! Put me *down!*

MEG: [*Calling*] Excuse me.

MUSICIANS: [*A crash, as though the* ZOOKEEPER *has been dropped*]

ZOOKEEPER: [*Off*] Ow. That wasn't funny.

ELEPHANT: [*Off*] [*Trumpeting laughs*]
[*The* ZOOKEEPER *enters, looking ruffled. He wears very heavy spectacles and carries a scrubbing brush*]

ZOOKEEPER: [*Rudely*] What is it? We're closed.

MEG: Sorry, but I wonder if you can help me?

ZOOKEEPER: I'm the one who needs help. Have you ever tried bathing an elephant?

MEG: No.

ZOOKEEPER: It's no joke.

ELEPHANT: [*Off*] [*Trumpeting*]

ZOOKEEPER: [*Shouting off*] Quiet! [*To* MEG]

Now clear off. We're closed.

MEG: But it's urgent.
[*As the* ZOOKEEPER *talks, an* ELEPHANT'S *trunk enters from behind the screen and grabs him round the body*]

ZOOKEEPER: So is the elephant's bath ... Aaaaah! [*He struggles with the trunk*] Let go! Aaaaah!

ELEPHANT: [*Off*] [*Trumpeting*]
[*The* ZOOKEEPER *struggles harder*]

ZOOKEEPER: There'll be no buns at bedtime. Aaaaah!
[*He is dragged off behind the screen, by the trunk*]

ELEPHANT: [*Off*] [*Trumpeting*]
[MEG *gives up for a while, and returns to look at the other* ANIMALS *in the cages upstage*]

ZOOKEEPER: [*Off*] Now settle down, Emily, please. You've got to have a bath. Good girl.

MUSICIANS: [*Struggling noises and rattling of bars*]

ZOOKEEPER: [*Off*] Stay, stay!

MUSICIANS: [*More struggling noises and rattling of bars*]

ZOOKEEPER: [*Off*] No, don't sit down. Please!

MUSICIANS: [*Crash — the sound of breaking glass*]

ZOOKEEPER: [*Off*] Oh no! You've broken them. You can go without buns for a week!

ELEPHANT: [*Off*] [*'It's not fair' trumpeting!*]
[*Enter the* ZOOKEEPER, *holding his shattered spectacles*]

ZOOKEEPER: They're ruined. And I can hardly see a thing without them.
[MEG *wanders down to meet him. The* ZOO-KEEPER *bumps into her and gets a big shock*]

Aaaaah!
[*He peers at* MEG]

I'm sorry. The elephant sat on me specs, you see, and I'm lost without them.

MEG: Oh dear. I am sorry. I was hoping you could help me.

ZOOKEEPER: How did you get in? The gate's locked.

MEG: I flew.

ZOOKEEPER: Flew?

MEG: I'm a witch.

ZOOKEEPER: A what?

MEG: No, a witch.

ZOOKEEPER: A witch. Good gracious. I've never met a witch before. What do you want?

MEG: I'm looking for a tiger.

ZOOKEEPER: Why, have you lost one?

MEG: No, no. I'm interested to see one. If you've got such a thing. Please.

ZOOKEEPER: Well, all right then. He's in there.

[*He points* MEG *towards the cage door stage left*]

He's called Stripy. But be careful. Dangerous animals, tigers.

[MEG *creeps to the cage. She peers in. All the other* ANIMALS *are watching*]

MEG: I can't see him.

ZOOKEEPER: He's probably asleep.

MEG: He's not in there.

ZOOKEEPER: What do you mean, he's not in there? He's . . .

[MEG *helps him towards the cage door. He peers in*]

ZOOKEEPER: [*Suddenly*] He's not in there! He's escaped! Help! Don't panic! Sound the alarm! The tiger's escaped! Stripy!

MUSICIANS: [*An alarm bell and possibly a wailing siren*]

ANIMALS: [*A babble of concerned noises*]
[*The* ZOOKEEPER *and* MEG *rush around in panic, bumping into each other*]

[*They exit: the* ZOOKEEPER *off right and* MEG *off left*]

STORYTELLER: [*Above the din*] Hearing the alarm, Mog came back, looking for Meg.
[*Enter* MOG *from stage right. He looks around, but cannot find* MEG]

Then the zookeeper came back.
[*The* ZOOKEEPER *returns and, peering hard, sees* MOG. *The alarm stops*]

ZOOKEEPER: *There* he is! There's my tiger. Come on, Stripy. Good cat. Good cat.
[*He starts backing the mystified* MOG *towards the cage by the stage-left screen*]

No one's going to hurt you. That's it. Good cat.
[MOG *backs into the cage. The* ZOOKEEPER *mimes locking it*]

Gotcha! And never try to escape again. I'll

get you something to eat, though you don't deserve it.
[*He exits, shortsightedly, right*]

[MEG *enters left, passing the cage*]

MEG: [*Calling*] Owl! Mog! Where are you?
[MEG *suddenly sees* MOG, *waving at her from the cage*]

There you are! Come out.
[*She tries to open the cage*]

It's locked! How did you get in there?

MOG: Miaow.
[*He mimes what has happened as the* STORY-TELLER *explains*]

STORYTELLER: Mog explained that the zoo-keeper locked him in, and Meg realized that because the elephant had broken the zoo-keeper's glasses, the zookeeper must have mistaken Mog for the tiger.

MOG: [*Nodding*] Miaow!

MEG: What are we going to do?

MUSICIANS: [*Idea ping*]
[MOG *mimes 'A spell'*]

MEG: Do a magic spell?
[MOG *nods*]

MEG: To get you out?
[MOG *nods*]

Tell you what. I'll go one better. I'll make you change places with the tiger. So the tiger will end up in the cage, safe and sound.

MOG: [*As if to say, 'What about me?'*] Miaow!

MEG: What about you? Well, you will find yourself wherever the tiger is *now*, and sniff your way back here. Right?
[MOG *nods, warily*]

Good. Stand by.
[*She puts down her broomstick and takes off her hat*]

MUSICIANS: [*Magic spell notes*]
[*The* ANIMALS *all nervously cover their eyes*]

[*As* MEG *chants the spell, she takes the ingredients from her cloak pocket and puts them in the hat. Then she waves her hand over the hat*]

MEG: [*Chanting*] Feather of raven
           Leg of a frog
           Make the tiger
           Swap with Mog!
[*The lights go out*]

MUSICIANS: [*Two whooshing noises to suggest the*

transposition]
   [*The lights come on again.* MOG *has disappeared.* OWL *is in the cage*]

STORYTELLER: But the spell went wrong.
   [*The* ANIMALS *uncover their eyes*]

ANIMALS: Booooo!

MEG: Aaaaaah! It's Owl. What are *you* doing in there?

OWL: Whoo! Whoo!
   [MEG *rushes to the cage, putting her hat back on*]

   [*The* ZOOKEEPER *enters with a bucket of tiger food*]

ZOOKEEPER: Here you are, Stripy. Come and get it! [*He sees* OWL] Who are you?

MEG: [*Embarrassed*] He's Owl.

ZOOKEEPER: Where's my tiger?

MEG: I don't know.

ZOOKEEPER: He was in there!

MEG: No he wasn't!

ZOOKEEPER: He was. I caught him.

MEG: No you didn't. That was Mog.

ZOOKEEPER: Mog?

MEG: My cat. Look, here he is!
[MOG *enters, dazed. He joins the group*]

ZOOKEEPER: But what's that owl doing in the cage?

MEG: I magicked him there. By mistake. Instead of your tiger.

ZOOKEEPER: [*Furiously*] So where's my tiger?

MEG: I don't know!
[*The* ZOOKEEPER *mimes unlocking the cage and opens it*]

ZOOKEEPER: Owl, out!
[OWL *emerges.* MEG *and* MOG *greet him*]

MEG: Owl, I'm sorry.

ZOOKEEPER: [*Calling*] Stripy! Stripy!
[*The* ZOOKEEPER *exits behind the stage-right screen*]

MEG: Maybe I should have used wing of bat instead of leg of frog. [*To* OWL] Are you all right?
[MEG *tries to comfort* OWL]

MUSICIANS: [*A dramatic rumble on a drum or keyboard*]
[*Slowly, unseen by* MEG, MOG *and* OWL, *the* TIGER *enters from stage right. He suddenly*

sees MEG, MOG *and* OWL *and reacts hungrily!*]

STORYTELLER: [*A loud whisper*] The tiger!

TIGER: Aha!
[MEG, MOG *and* OWL *turn and see him*]

MEG: Aaaaah!

OWL: Ooooo!

MOG: Miaow!

MUSICIANS: [*Exciting chase music*]
[*The* TIGER *chases* MEG, MOG *and* OWL *round and round. The chase should be controlled, not too fast, with small, energetic steps*]

ANIMALS: [*Chanting*] Chase! Chase! Chase! Chase!
[*After several circuits,* MOG *stops and turns to confront the* TIGER. MEG *and* OWL *hide*]

[MOG *and the* TIGER *prowl round each other*]

MUSICIANS: [*Dramatic rumble*]
[MOG *gets himself into the right position, so that when the* TIGER *suddenly pounces,* MOG *sidesteps. The* TIGER *dashes past him straight into the cage*]

[MEG *dashes out and mimes locking the cage.* MOG *and* OWL *join her*]

ANIMALS: Hooray!

MEG: Gotcha!

TIGER: What? [*Realizing*] It was a tiger trap. [*Suddenly laughing*] Oh, well played! Fooled me fair and square! Ha ha ha.

MEG: [*Surprised*] Aren't you annoyed? Being locked up again?

TIGER: No, no. I like it here. First-class service. Lots of visitors. Ideal home for a retired tiger.

MEG: Retired? You don't look old enough to be retired.

TIGER: You're too kind. I'm still fairly frisky when given the chance! Which reminds me, thank you for that lovely game.

MEG: Game?

TIGER: All that chasing about. Splendid sport. Haven't enjoyed myself so much for years. Jolly decent of you.

MEG: We didn't realize it was a game – we were terrified!

OWL: [*Agreeing*] Oooooh!

TIGER: Terrified? Of yours truly?

MEG: Yes. Tigers are . . . well . . . not noted for being cuddly.

TIGER: There's no need to be frightened of me. I'm long in the tooth. Past my prime.
[OWL *bobs up and down, miming 'tooth'*]

OWL: Whoo! Whoo!

MEG: What? Oh yes! [*To the* TIGER] Er . . . talking of teeth . . .

TIGER: What teeth?

MEG: Your teeth.

TIGER: Oh! Ha ha ha ha! I'm so ancient, all my teeth have dropped out!

MEG: You mean you're a toothless tiger?

TIGER: Exactly. Long in the tooth, short in the teeth! Ha ha ha.

MEG: Oh dear.

TIGER: Doesn't worry me. Saves cleaning them.

MEG: No, I mean, 'Oh dear, we were hoping you could help us.'

TIGER: How?

MEG: We're looking for a tiger's tooth. For my magic spells.

TIGER: Mmm. Listen. My very last tooth dropped out only yesterday . . .

OWL: Oooooh!

MOG: [*As if to say, 'Where is it?'*] Miaow?

MEG: Mog's saying, 'Where is it?'

TIGER: Under my pillow. Waiting for the fairies to collect it.

MEG: Do you think I could have it?

TIGER: Are you a fairy?

MEG: Well, no. But I am a witch.

TIGER: The fairies always leave ten p.

MEG: [*Thinking quickly*] Witches leave eleven p.

TIGER: Fair enough. If it's still there, you shall have it.

MEG: Thank you.
[*The* TIGER *exits to look*]

TIGER: [*Off*] Bingo!
[*He returns, with the tooth*]

Here it is.
[*He gives the tooth to* MEG. MEG *gives him the money, which he examines with great pleasure*]

MEG: Thank you!
  [*She carefully puts the tooth in her pocket*]

TIGER: Thank *you*!
  [*The* ZOOKEEPER *enters from stage right, carrying the tiger food*]

ZOOKEEPER: [*Calling*] Stripy! Stripy!

MEG: It's all right, Zookeeper. We've found him.

ZOOKEEPER: Really?
  [*He shortsightedly goes to the cage, bumping into it on arrival*]
  Stripy, is that you?
  [*The* TIGER *nods*]

  It is! You're a naughty boy, but I'm glad to see you. Here's a bite to eat.
  [*He mimes unlocking the door and enters the cage, to leave the tiger food*]

  [*The* TIGER *briefly pops out, unseen by the* ZOOKEEPER]

TIGER: [*To* MEG, MOG *and* OWL] See what I mean? Friendly staff! First-class service!
  [*The* TIGER *pops back into the cage, still unseen by the* ZOOKEEPER]

ZOOKEEPER: [*Leaving the cage and walking straight past* MEG, MOG *and* OWL] Thank you all so much for finding him.
  [*He bumps into a screen*]

ZOOKEEPER: Where are you?

MEG: Here we are.

ZOOKEEPER: Oh, sorry. I'm lost without my specs.

MEG: Tell you what. I'll mend them for you. By magic.

ZOOKEEPER: Good gracious. Will you really?

MEG: I'll have a try. I must get *one* spell right today.

ZOOKEEPER: I've got all the pieces.
[*He takes them from his pocket. They are wrapped in the magic handkerchief*]

MEG: Good. Can I borrow your hanky?

ZOOKEEPER: Of course.
[*He gives it to her*]

MEG: [*Holding the hanky by the 'magic' corner, and bringing the other corners to meet it*]
One, two, three,
Pop them in and you will see.
[*The ZOOKEEPER drops the pieces in the secret pocket*]

MUSICIANS: [*Magic notes*]

MEG: [*Chanting*] Tweezers and squeezers

Pinches and pecks
Abracadabra
Mend these old specs!
[*She takes the hanky by the 'magic' corner and one other, and flaps the hanky. The pieces have disappeared*]

MUSICIANS: [*Whooshing noises*]

MEG: Here you are! Oh no! The pieces have disappeared!

ANIMALS: Booooo!

MEG: Please. Everyone help. Say after me.

MUSICIANS: [*Magic notes*]

MEG: Tweezers and squeezers

ALL [*Including the* ANIMALS *and the audience*]: Tweezers and squeezers

MEG: Pinches and pecks

ALL: Pinches and pecks

MEG: Abracadabra

ALL: Abracadabra

MEG: Mend these old specs!

ALL: Mend these old specs!
   [*The lights go out*]

MUSICIANS: [*Whooshing noises*]
   [*The lights came on again*]

   [*The* ZOOKEEPER *is wearing his mended glasses*]

STORYTELLER: The spell worked!

OWL: [*Pointing at the glasses*] Ooooo! Ooooo!

ZOOKEEPER: [*Realizing*] You did it. [*Looking around*] Thank you. They're perfect!

MEG: I got a spell right!

ALL [*Including the* ANIMALS]: Hooray!

MUSICIANS: [*Triumphant fanfare*]

STORYTELLER: The end.